The Power
of True
Forgiveness

We took an Oath

The Power
of True
Forgiveness

We took an Oath

Suzette Grant-Walker

Tamarind Hill Press
www.tamarindhillpress.co.uk

THANK YOU

I especially want to say thank you for purchasing and reading my book. Without a doubt, I know that your lives will be transformed through the power of God's love and the pages of this book. Let me also take this opportunity to say thank you for sharing and spreading the word about the Power of True Forgiveness with your friends and family as I know you will; this is highly appreciated.

Leaving a review and telling your friend where the Power of True Forgiveness can be bought or buying them a copy would be a gift treasured for a lifetime. You never know how many lives you will touch by this one kind gesture. Your review enables me to become a better author and helps others in finding my book and gaining from it as I hope that you have.

Let us keep in touch...
Get to know Suzette Grant-Walker better by visiting her website:
www.suzettegwalker.com
Follow on Instagram
@suzie_walker23

For business:

Email
Suzettegrant1571@gmail.com
suzettegrant1571@yahoo.com

Phone
+1 954-934-4327

Publisher
info@tamarindhillpress.co.uk

DEDICATION

To my husband, Clifton A. Walker, for his love and support over the years. If I had to do it all over again, I would still choose you.

To my sisters and brothers for their belief in me; even when I could not believe in myself.

MY INSPIRATION

Ms. Elethea Lyn, my best friend affectionately called Cindy, whose life inspired me. Having step children of her own that she took in, loved, nourished and raised. When I look at her life, I took courage and told myself that if she did it, then so could I. She is truly a mother and a role model. Thank God for you Cindy, I love you.

FOREWORD

Some years ago, I read an article in *Psychology Today* entitled: '6 Important facts about forgiveness.' Fact number 6 stated: "Choosing Forgiveness can be an act of Empowerment."

In defence of that, the author, Melanie Greenberg, wrote: "Forgiveness can mean continuing to work for good and be a loving person, even when faced with abhorrent deeds. This can send a personal message that love is stronger than hate and fear." How does the victim of violated trust boldly state that love is stronger than hate and fear? The victim does it by acknowledging God at work through the power of the Holy Spirit. Allowing ourselves to be empowered through forgiveness is clearly the message presented in **The Power of True Forgiveness**.

I have been privileged to know the author, Pastor Suzette Walker, for 15 years. We met at a Church we both attended in Fort Lauderdale, and since 2014, we have been serving together at the same Church, Building Believers Worship Center, North Lauderdale, FL. Pastor Walker has earned the right to speak about forgiveness from a personal perspective and experience. On a journey which shook the foundation of her marriage and sought to disentangle years of what some would have called marital bliss–we are as if in a court of law, where the most credible witness is an eyewitness–Pastor

Walker gives invaluable, unscripted facts about the case for forgiveness by presenting clear evidence of her life as a married, Christian woman who faced the unthinkable violation of trust. As a first-hand witness, she provides undisputable testimony about what she saw, felt and heard when her marriage ran into trouble.

Painstakingly, she invites her readers to take the journey with her down the path of infidelity, where she bravely shares in detail and at length what hurt, pain, anger and trust betrayed looked and felt like. The complexity of the case is even more dynamic because her personal perspective is that she is a woman who boldly and authoritatively teaches and preaches forgiveness. Her life experience had taken her to a place where she had to question the truth of what she had believed for years and the possibility of real or true forgiveness.

Is it conceivable that love is strong enough to forgive one of the worst of offences? Is love stronger than hate and fear? Timely pealing back one layer after another, Pastor Walker takes us through: infidelity; the struggles to forgive; her innermost feelings; the beginnings of the healing process and finally how she knew she was healed. She is faithful to the belief that, "there is a sanctity in marriage and if we place God at the center of our marriages, then our marriages would be what God has ordained it to be."

The book speaks candidly to married couples (but is not limited to married couples) who may be facing the issue of forgiveness. It adds an important reminder that forgiveness is not to be viewed in degrees; we must use a broad-brush stroke in applying forgiveness because forgiveness is not based on the offence, it covers all offences.

I believe the message in this book has been presented clearly and is an important one for the World at large, the Christian Church in general, and married couples. There is a major reason why this book is important: unforgiveness is detrimental, specifically to the one who needs to offer forgiveness because of the possible long term social, physical, emotional and spiritual implications of unforgiveness. This is a must read, and the takeaway must be that there is no story in the chapter of your life that the healing waters of forgiveness cannot reach. To quote the author: "Forgiveness is a process and is beneficial to the person who was wronged more than the person who did the wrong."

Beverley Harvey
Executive Pastor, BBWC
North Lauderdale, FL

ACKNOWLEDGEMENTS

Firstly, to the inspiration of the Holy Spirit, who delivered me from the power of unforgiveness and has brought everything back to my memory as if it all happened yesterday; thank you. Secondly, to my husband Clifton A. Walker who is my biggest fan and supporter, thank you. You are the love of my life, my first and only love; no one has the power to love or hurt me more than you, and today I celebrate you honey; we did it. My forever love, my darling son Jon-Ross Walker, thank you for believing in my ability to write this book. I have watched you mature before my very eyes and I am proud of you, son. Special recognition to my new-born baby, Jhireh Esther-Jade Walker, who was sick at this time but still allowed mommy to write. I bless and thank God for daddy who took care of you for me.

To a beautiful young woman who is fast becoming one of my favourite persons, Pastor Beverley Harvey; you inspired me and encouraged me to write while I felt the passion to. Barbara Grant, my sister, who knew the truth all along and kept it hidden to protect me; I love you sis. It would be remiss of me not to say thanks to my brother Oliver Grant and his wife Ann Grant for their love and support given in the very early stages of my pain. Thank you both for loving me and protecting me as best as you could. To my niece, Tesha Grant – who I affectionately call *T* – who cried with me on so many occasions; I cannot forget the day when we were home alone and I had that experience with God and you said to me later, "Aunty, I was so afraid for you because I did not know what to do." I love you T.

To Shirley Gibson and Ieasha Whittaker who stood with me in it all and kept telling me God would get me through this, thank you. To my girl Carol Beadle, I bless God for you every day; you have touched my life in so many ways that I cannot say thanks enough. My prayer for you is that He will heal you in every area of your life and you will be all that God wants you to be. Last, but never the least, my sister from another mother, Miriam Lee; girl, you are my ride or die, my prayer partner and my outlet when I want to vent. Thank you for seeing me in so many different lights and loving all my imperfections; I love you.

God bless you all. Thank you all for touching my life in ways that only each of you could. I love all of you so much.

GLOSSARY

[1] Baby-mother – The mother of a

man's child(ren).

[2] I would draw for you – I would date

you.

Table of Contents

INTRODUCTION

Many times we try to run away from confronting the trials that come our way, and try-by all means-to either avoid or suppress dealing with our difficulties. I have come to know that one cannot defeat what one will not confront. David had to face his Goliath, Daniel the lions, and Jesus the cross. The Power of True Forgiveness is really based on the infallible Word of God.

What is forgiveness really? Many people will say, "I forgive you," but will still hold on to the anger and the pain. Some will never have a relationship with you again. My belief is totally different and that is why I titled this book, *The Power of True Forgiveness.*

I believe the story told in the book of Genesis about Joseph forgiving his brothers is one of the most powerful stories on forgiveness in the Bible.

Joseph not only forgave his brothers for the wrong they did him, but he also embraced them as if they had never hurt him. He recognized that his brothers' actions were meant for evil, but God used them for his good. Like Joseph, do not be bound by the events that brought you there, lift your hands and say, "Lord thank You." We never know the future, but God does. Sometimes the path that leads us into our destiny is painful but when we get there, we will be able to look back and say it was all worth it. Tony Evans teaches that forgiveness pulls you closer not push you apart or away.

What if Jesus forgave us and decided He no longer wants anything to do with us? How terrible would that be, yet isn't this how some of us forgive? I call this "forgiveness with conditions." Now, hopefully you're beginning to understand the title of this book is entitled.

So, how do we define true forgiveness? In my own experience and opinion this would be my definition: True forgiveness means letting go of the hurt, the bitterness, the malice and moving forward without the pain of the past. Accepting your loved ones as though you have never been hurt. According to the Free online Dictionary, forgiveness is defined as: The renunciation of your right to punish or fight back against a person who has done you wrong and the granting of pardon and reconciliation. With the dictionary's definition the most important word is reconciliation, and this means restoration; restoring relations. This is what Joseph displayed in the Bible. He didn't forgive his brother's sins then forgot them. He embraced them and moved forward with them as brothers, with no ill will on his part. That is true forgiveness. It's not enough to say, "I forgive you but I won't forget," or "I forgive you, but I want nothing to do with you." I'm not saying that extending true forgiveness is easy, because it's not. What I am saying is that it is possible and with God we all have it in us to learn to truly forgive those who hurt us. It's also freeing.

Journey with me as I take you through the process of having to deal with unforgiveness. This book talks about finding out that infidelity was also involved in my marriage which led me to the struggles I faced to forgive. I open up about the phone confrontations, his excuses, me thinking I had to get even, my journey in the healing process and finally, how I knew I was healed.

I learnt the hard way that forgiveness is a process that does not happen overnight, and it will take the power of the Almighty God at work in your life to bring this about. I not only had to forgive my husband for committing adultery but also to accept a child and call him my own. As a Christian woman I knew I had to forgive my husband and everyone else involved, including myself, but it is far easier said than done. In my heart I felt I had forgiven but the old saying, "I will forgive but I will never forget," kept ringing true. The human nature that we possess, I believe, will enable us to forgive but to forget that's impossible; that is the reality. Once our minds learn something, we can't truly unlearn it. But how do we forgive and move on without being haunted by the memories? How do we keep the memories from pulling us back to that bitter place where unforgiveness lives?

Ultimately, it took the power of the Almighty God to get me to where I am today. I could not have done it in my own strength. No matter how hard I tried or how badly I wanted it, I kept going back to the pain of feeling less than a woman, the feelings of not being good enough, the question of why did he do it, until God delivered me through it and from the ugliness of unforgiveness.

Unforgiveness is ugly and it eats away at you. It eats at your heart and eventually your relationships with others. It is a baggage you do not want to carry around; it is an extra piece that is heavy and weighs you down like none other. God, I give you praise!

Let us think for a moment. I mentioned this earlier; what if God forgave us with those same principles that we forgive each other with? Imagine God said, "I will forgive that you have sinned against me, but I will never forget your sins." I want you to think on that and truly realise what this would mean but also what it means or does to the people we love when we say it. Haven't we all at one point or another sought forgiveness from one another or from God. I for one am so glad that, "If we confess our sins, He is faithful and just and will forgive us our sins and purify us from all unrighteousness" St John 1-9.

Micah 7:19 states, "You will again have compassion on us; you will tread our sins underfoot and hurl all our iniquities into the depths of the sea."

Forgiveness comes only from God and He has given us the power and the will to forgive others. This means that we are just as capable of forgiving each other without conditions. We might not be able to forget, but we do not have to keep living in that painful place of unforgiveness.

Remember, Matthew 6:14-15 says, "For if you forgive other people when they sin against you, your heavenly Father will also forgive you. But if you do not forgive others their sins, your Father will not forgive your sins."

I chose to be more like my Father. I chose to forgive and free myself from the depths of unforgiveness.

"Shattered, but I'm not broken
Wounded, but time will heal...
...Trials, they come to make me strong
I must endure, I must hold on..."

\- Yolanda Adams (Yet Still I Rise)

"It was the words of God coming to fruition in my life; he will fail if I fail."

CHAPTER ONE

The Journey Begins

"I just can't give up now, I've come too far from where I started from, nobody told me, the road would be easy, and I don't believe He's brought me this far, to leave me."

- Mary Mary

I met my husband a year after leaving high school in the year 1989, and I immediately took a liking to him. He dressed well, had a charming personality and he always made me laugh. We dated for nine years, then I became pregnant with our firstborn Jon-Ross in 1995. Life was pretty good with my family. I gave my heart to the Lord in 1996, then we decided to take our relationship a step further and we got married in 1997.

This journey that we are about to embark on, all started when my husband went to the United States of America in 2002. He kept cancelling his return trip home until he ran out of time. He had now overstayed his visitor's visa, and had he returned home, his visa would have been revoked and he would be denied re-entry to the US in the future. He was now unable to return home without repercussions and he was away from his family. Under the law, he also stood the chance of being deported and having his visa revoked. I began to pray this prayer of standing in the gap for him, not understanding the full meaning behind it. Later on, I learned through the revelation of the Holy Spirit what this meant, and it totally blew my mind.

I heard the voice of the Holy Spirit speak to my spirit so clearly saying, "Standing in the gap means that whatever temptation will present itself to him, will come to you first. Whatever test you pass, he'll pass and whatever test you fail, he'll fail." Little did I know what was about to unfold in our lives.

The best way I can describe the statement, "Standing in the gap," for the one who have not yet accepted Christ, would be like an individual who would go to any given length or measure to protect the ones they love from getting into trouble. In other words, they would desire to face the danger head on, rather than allow the danger to come to the ones they love.

Psalm 106:23 states, "So He said he would destroy them – had not Moses, his chosen one, stood in the breach before him to keep his wrath from destroying them." When I got that message, I knew I had to pray for my husband like I have never prayed before. Remember though, the message said, he'll pass the test if I pass it and will fail if I failed.

If anyone told me I would be challenged in my Christian faith the way I was, I would not have believed them. I was doing fine with him being away and my walk of faith in God was steadfast. Eventually I started drifting away from the things of God but it did not happen overnight. I am a licensed cosmetologist and worked on a plaza with other business owners. The young women who worked in their stores started patronizing my business and I now became their hairdresser. It was the start of drifting away from God.

My downward spiral in my faith began so innocently. Little by little I was becoming influenced by my clients' lifestyle; not suddenly but slowly over a period of two years. My life was rather bland. I was a church girl. Before my husband migrated we would hang out together, we had our regular night date, we enjoyed going to the movies together, we drove for miles to watch our favourite soccer team's games; I had fun with him and our son. I had everything going on. My life revolved around my family.

The Christian girlfriends I had were unmarried and were caught up in their own world as I was caught up in mine. The only other girlfriend I had was not a Christian and she too was caught up in her with her own life. Cindy was so busy raising her children, so we never went out together. We were both too busy being moms. My new business owner friends were involved with a social club that required them supporting other's events. They would cook food, sell liquor and have a drink out. At first, I would buy my meal in support of my friends, say my goodbyes and then get in my car and drive home. Then one night I decided I was going to hang out with them at one of their events.

I was slowly getting involved with the wrong crowd, rather than taking a Godly stand like when I started working there. I was letting my guard down. I was still attending Church, still working in the Church but I was no longer as dedicated to the things of God as I was accustomed to. I was not reading my Bible as much either. I realized that I was slacking off. It was as though I was seeking acceptance from the wrong crowd and was not as strong in my faith as when my husband left.

James 1:14 states, "But each person is tempted when they are dragged away by their own evil desire and enticed." Remembering this scripture, I now knew I was in trouble because my walk in

Christendom had become shaky and I wasn't living up to the standards of God's word as I should have been. It never happened overnight. It took a few years for me to find out how I would face the consequences of not walking worthy in my faith.

I loved my husband dearly and he loved me very much. We would frequently have this conversation which always ended like this, "I will never forgive you if you cheated and brought another child into our marriage. That would be the end of this." At the time, we had only one son, Jon-Ross J. Walker. Little did I know and understand the power of the spoken word and voicing my insecurities out loud. I found out much, much later that my husband was caught up in adultery.

Johnny, as he is affectionately called, had gotten involved with a young woman which turned out to be one serious affair. It was the words of God coming to fruition in my life; he will fail if I fail. Now, here's a lesson for you: sin is sin in God's eyes and there are things married people should just not do. As for me, I messed around to a point; meaning, I flirted and enjoyed the attention I was given by some men. After all, I was a catch. I owned my own business, drove a nice car and I was a beautiful chocolate skin girl. I did not get intimately involved with anyone at first, until I met this young man who I really began to take a liking to. He made me laugh and I was especially enjoying his attention more than the other men. He lived north of where I worked, and on almost every occasion he got, he would stop by my salon. He was friendly, and all the young women on the shopping centre liked him. He kept asking me to go out with him and I finally accepted his invitation; only due to loneliness and boredom. Before I knew it, I too had fallen into adultery.

Please journey with me as the plot thickens. I was now beginning to understand the challenges before me and the vow I had made to stand for my husband. For you to truly understand, we have to go back to the beginning. With my parents being

Christians, Church for me was a must. From a young age, I was exposed to the knowledge of God. We had what we called then our Sunday School Classes, and I must truly say I was very much involved in what we did in our classes. At about age thirteen, I started teaching one of these classes because the Word of God really intrigued me. I learned the Bible stories, and won many awards as most outstanding Sunday school student. This went on until I was seventeen years old. I totally stopped attending church when my mother got sick. As mentioned earlier, nine years later I gave my heart to the Lord, by then a mother and unmarried.

As mentioned earlier, I got married to my son's father. After dating for six years, we decided to rent an apartment together and we were together for another two years before I became his wife. Yes, we vowed to be true to each other forsaking all else until death do us part. Then our journey began.

After he migrated, I never saw him again until almost two years later. When I finally did, his behaviour was not as welcoming as I had hoped. I thought it was kind of strange, but I couldn't put my finger on the reason for the change. I guessed not being together for a while we had somehow lost that kind of intimacy, but I was extremely glad to see him. He was an extrovert, he loved partying and having a good time and when he attended these parties he would come home in the wee hours of the morning. This kind of behaviour brought doubts into my mind about his faithfulness and I started to have feelings of insecurities. This already started back home in the islands but I never had any proof of any infidelity.

On one of my visits, I remember finding a picture of a young woman hidden in his wallet telling him, "I love you." He lied his way out of it saying this girl gave them to all her friends. I was not convinced but I gave him the benefit of the doubt because he tore it up in front of me. Yet somehow this experience had always been vivid in the back of my mind. Ladies, I must say this; our husbands will do anything to try and assure us they are faithful to cover their tracks. Well this was the first clue of what was really to come for me.

One thing I must make known is that my husband has always been a good husband, father and provider. I was never verbally or physically abused by him. Yet still, what I went through emotionally and spiritually when the proof of infidelity raised its ugly head was terrifying.

*"**I** secretly blamed myself for his affair."*

CHAPTER TWO

Infidelity

"Life is easy when you're up on the mountain
You got peace of mind like you've never known
but things change when you are down in the valley
don't lose faith cause you're never alone."
                               -   Lynda Randle

I started traveling to and from to be with my husband every chance I got, Easter breaks and summer holidays mostly – because our son was out of school and we could spend time together as a family. By then I no longer felt the distance between us. We were once again, in my mind, the perfect little family although separated by distance. I made frequent trips in between because I had this need to be with him. As time progressed, we started making plans to once again live as a family without all the traveling back and forth.

Then, in the year 2004, our plans and our lives were suddenly disrupted. Johnny had a child with someone else. The thing I feared the most had come true; he had a child in our marriage. Up until that point I still had no knowledge of him having an affair much less a child! Even though I had my suspicions that he might have been seeing someone, because of the way he screened his calls when he was in my presence, I had no proof.

My car was in the shop one day and I needed to make my way home from the salon by other means. On this particular evening, I decided that I would walk home because I lived like fifteen minutes from where I worked. On my way home, I remember deciding to stop briefly at a friend's house just to chit chat, when my greatest fear caught up with me. She told me my husband had a child and that my in-laws all knew about it. My friend explained that he had sent them pictures and they were all displayed over my mother-in-law's dressing table.

I couldn't believe what she was saying, I wanted to die. She saw the look of disbelief on my face and started saying some negative things about his family that I won't get into in this book. I guess It was supposed to make me feel better, but all I wanted to do was crawl into a hole and die. I felt my supposedly perfect little family crashing in. Funny, I did not break down in front of her, but I hurriedly left. As I rounded the corner from her house, the tears started coming down uncontrollably. Unconsciously blinded by my tears, I was walking in the middle of the street and was not aware of it until I heard the honking of car horns that jolted me back to reality. Drivers that I knew pulled over wanting to know if I was okay, and as much as I could hardly think straight; with tears streaming down my face, I told them I was fine.

The phone confrontation

I felt betrayed. I felt as if my legs would fail me. I felt numb. I prayed the information I had just received was false. She did not hear correctly. Someone was lying, and I could not wait to hear the truth from my husband. He would not lie to me. My fears were not going to become a reality; God would not do this to me.

I called Johnny hysterically and I asked the question, "Do you have a child?"

He answered, "No."

I remember saying, "Do not even think of lying to me, because I just heard that there are also pictures that you have sent to your mom to prove it."

He paused for a while then he answered, "Yes."

My next question was, "Is it a girl?" Because I had made up my mind that I was going to have another child and I wanted the baby to be a girl. So, as much as I wasn't prepared for a stepchild, now that one was present, I certainly didn't want it to be a girl. Fortunately, it was a boy. Heartbroken and not knowing what this knowledge was going to do to our marriage, he started apologizing for hurting me. I hung up on him and walked home. After talking with him, I called my sisters to tell them the news and three of my four sisters came over.

You see, what I didn't mention before is that I am the baby in the family. So they have always tried in their own ways to protect me in every way possible. One of my sisters, Barbara, who is mentioned in my acknowledgement, knew of the child a year before but had not said a word to me. She would always ask, as I recall coming home from visiting with my husband, if everything was okay. Whenever she did, I thought that was just what families do. My big sister was simply checking up on me. When I asked why she hadn't told me, she said she didn't have the heart to see me fall apart or play any part in the break-up of my marriage, should I be unable to handle this truth.

My sisters stayed with me way into the night and I remember telling them that if I lived to see the break of the new day, I would be okay. Easier said than done. I felt my whole world crashing in.

The next person I contacted was one of my in-laws. She and my husband, her brother, had a good relationship and she was also the only one of my in-laws that I felt really cared for me and I cared for her too. At the time, her mother never really cared for the young man she was dating, just as she never cared for me, so I think that similar situation kind of drew us together. We were kind of cool. Well, she blatantly lied over the phone and said the information was not true even after her brother admitted it to me that it was. Of this she had no knowledge. She later told me that she could not have told me for the very same reason my sister gave. I felt no anger towards her or my sister; I just had a feeling of numbness. In their own way, they were both protecting the people they love.

The next person I had to face, was my son, Jon-Ross, "Jay," as he is affectionately called. This tore me up. He got in from school, saw the tears and asked, "Mommy what's wrong?" I told him that his daddy had another family and was taken aback by his next question which was, "Are you going to leave him?" To which he answered himself, "No! Let daddy leave the other woman," with tears streaming down his face. Remembering this has brought back tears to my eyes. All I could do was hug him so close because I had no clue as to how all this was going to work out.

My husband kept calling to find out how I was doing but I never felt much like talking to him. My sisters left after a long while but all throughout that night sleep had evaded me and by the late hours I could hardly see through my eyes. Morning came and I was still alive. I somehow knew then that whatever the outcome, my son and I would be okay.

I remember making a call to my mother-in-law the following day. I wasn't expecting much sympathy from her because I learned a long time before, and in my marriage, that I was one of her least favourite persons. I made the call anyway, hoping this time around she would be nice and wouldn't be sarcastic. Our conversation was very short.

"Good morning Mrs. Walker. I heard your son has sent you pictures of your grandson."

Her response in these exact words was, "You're the one going back and forth to America all the time, you should know."

Very calmly, I said to her, "This is between Johnny and I and we will work it out."

I truly loved Johnny and because I did, I made a promise never ever to be disrespectful to his mom out of respect for him, so I hung up my phone. Oh, the anger boiled in me, but the control that the Holy Spirit had on me was simply amazing.

Payback

After that conversation with his mom I wanted to get even with Johnny. I wanted to throw in his face that I also had slept with someone else, but I was careful not to get pregnant. What was he thinking; how could he do this to us? You see, there were men who wanted me to give them a chance in my life and yes, I messed up too, but my affair was not serious enough to give my marriage up for it. Still I felt like I was dealt a hand that I was sure going to lose with. I had crossed the boundaries and I somehow felt that God was getting back at me for the stance I did not take. He told me to stand in the gap for him and I did not obey. I failed both God and Johnny so miserably.

Feeling so hurt, in my mind, now was the perfect time to get even but I wanted to hear what he had to say for himself. My blood was boiling.

I knew I had to see Johnny as soon as possible, so I started making plans to visit him. The thing is, I have never envisioned myself living without him; he was my world. As much as I owned my own business, he took care of us financially and I was afraid that something could go wrong and I was fearful of starting over. I wasn't ready to just throw in the towel. We had a family and a life together.

Before Johnny, I dated once, just once. I had just gotten out of high school and wanted, like every other young girl I knew then, to say I had a boyfriend. I thought I had fallen head over heels in love but that didn't last long. Let me call him Ned. He met my parents, I knew some of his family and we dated for a few months. During this time, I met my husband. I took a liking to him immediately but he knew I was seeing Ned and he too was otherwise involved. We chitchatted but nothing serious happened until we started communicating on a more serious level. I began to see less and less of Ned until I finally broke it off with him.

Interestingly though, my husband was never the kind of guy I wanted to marry. He was not as tall as I would like him to be, not as handsome as my fine brothers or Ned, but he made me laugh and I liked him. I must say, I never cheated on Ned with my husband. I made a clean break. Of course, my mother wasn't pleased with my decision and gave my husband-to-be a hard time in the beginning of our relationship. Oh, she made him have it. Like Ned, he was not allowed to enter our house—we had to talk at the gate—but his winning personality won her over and she later grew to love and respect him so much. Johnny could do no wrong in her eyes. I sometimes wondered how she would have reacted to the news of his infidelity had she still been alive.

I had never missed my mom more than I did then. She was my mentor, my friend, my confidant; she was a woman of great wisdom and insight, and man did I need Godly wisdom at the time. My mother was a stalwart in the Christian faith, and I am so grateful that I grew up in a Christian home. I would hear her constant prayers growing up and saw the love she had not just for her children but my father's children as well. They both had children prior to meeting each other, and so my father became a father to her children, and she became a mother to his. If there was anyone I needed to comfort me and tell me that everything was going to be alright it was my mom. I loved her dearly and at her passing I believed a part of me died. After my mom's passing, I sought for a mother in my mother-in-law but I never found one and my husband can attest to this fact.

You see, relationship-wise I was unlearned in a lot of ways, so Johnny taught me mostly everything I knew about making love. There were so many conflicting emotions that I was dealing with and even though I never said this openly to anyone until now, I secretly blamed myself for his affair. What if I had remained faithful to him and God, would God not have kept His Word as promised? Yes, He would; but I did not keep my end of the bargain. I thought no one will ever understand why I would not just take the easy way and walk away but deep within me I wanted my husband.

I recall going to my then pastor and sharing the news of my husband's infidelity, that resulted in the birth of a child. He listened and with very comforting words said to me, "Suzette, it is when you are crushed that you know what you are made of." Who wants to hear that when their heart is bleeding? It took a while for me to understand the true meaning behind it. My understanding of that phrase is that; anything that is crushed, whatever flows from it, is what it consists of. If you are bitter, angry, or jealous on the inside, those same emotions would become an outward reflection. Likewise, if you're kind, loving, and gentle on the inside it will also flow on the outside. I was deeply hurt but I still loved him so much, and if he wanted me, I would fight for my marriage.

Matthew 19:9 states, "And I say unto you, whosoever shall put away his wife, except it be for fornication, and shall marry another, committeth adultery: and whoso marrieth her which is put away doth commit adultery."

Proverbs 6:32 also speaks on this saying, "[But] whoso commits adultery with a woman lacketh understanding: He that doeth it destroyeth his own soul." So here through biblical reference I had just cause to divorce Johnny. Then my pastor told me that if I could find it in my heart to forgive him then I should do so and work it out.

1st Corinthians 7:15-16 says, "[15]But if the unbeliever leaves, let it be so. The brother or the sister is not under bondage in such circumstances; God has called us to live in peace. [16]How do you know, wife, whether you will save your husband? Or how do you know, husband, whether you will save your wife?"

My husband did not know God as his personal Savior yet; I was the believing wife. At the time, I did not know whether my husband wanted our marriage. I wasn't sure if he was going to continue with his affair and make the mother of his child his next wife. So as much as I was still so much in love with him, the ball was in his court. There was one promise I mad myself; I would never have the knowledge of unfaithfulness in my marriage and settle for it. It is one thing not to be aware of a situation but to be aware and settle for it is where I have a personal problem. If he chose to walk away it would have torn me to pieces, but I had made up my mind that I would rather lose him than to settle for his disrespect.

I am a Certified Nursing Assistant and I have seen the different kinds of abuse that one can encounter and have seen the many devastating effect it has had on women and children and I was not going to settle for that. As a Clergy member I have also counselled couples who were miserable in their marriages, but to save face, they were enduring the torture of staying together rather than seeking the help they needed to make their marriages better. Although I had my insecurities dealing with, I was not willing to settle for anything less than having the total respect of my husband. I left my pastor's office with the hope that things would work in my favour. My husband and I kept communicating and he was reassuring me that he loved me and the affair was not that serious. But he was not sounding very convincing at all. We were talking about him having an affair that resulted in a child.

Finally the day came, and I bought my ticket and decided, figuratively speaking, "now is the time to take the bull by the horn." I had to now confront him face to face and meet the then almost two-year-old child and his mother. I was not looking forward to this. Fortunately, he was living with my brother and his family, so I had their support. I knew I needed to have someone in my corner should this meeting not turn out the way I was hoping it would, in my favour, of course. I must say this; before learning of the child, I often had dreams of Johnny cheating and at one point the description of who he was cheating with was so profound. When I shared all this with him, he denied everything, but the plot was about to unravel itself.

God in times, past and up until present, always forewarns his people of impending doom. It is either we obey or turn a deaf ear to it and not heed his warning but He has always warned. Let me give one example of being forewarned. In the days of Noah when God told him to build an ark the people had never seen rain, yet out of obedience to God he built it; amidst the mockery and jeers he built.

Genesis 6:13-14 states, "[13]And God said to Noah, "I have determined to make an end of all flesh, for the earth is filled with violence through them. Behold, I will destroy them with the earth. [14]Make yourself an ark, of gopher wood; make rooms in the ark and cover it inside and out with pitch." Taking heed of God's warning, he built and preached. Eventually the ark was completed and the rains came, and only Noah, his family and the animals that he was instructed to bring in were saved. The entire earth was destroyed by the flood. My message to you is to listen and take heed before you have to deal with the consequences of your disobedience.

"*It was never a real relationship.*"

CHAPTER THREE

The Struggles to Forgive

I arrived at the airport and Johnny was there waiting to pick me up. I had seen him three months prior to this trip and he looked so different this time around. He was much thinner and looked awfully fatigued and stressed out (no exaggeration there). We said hello, he took my bags, got into the car and then the tears came streaming down again. I felt so cold and distant towards him. There wasn't the usual embrace or familiarity between us; just silence, uncomfortable silence. We were like total strangers.

Finally, he asked how I was doing and very coldly I answered, "You have eyes, can't you see?" Not much was said after that. We arrived at my brother's house and we went in. He went to our room, and I went to my sister-in-law's room. I was a real mess; no words of comfort could warm my broken heart. I just kept on crying.

That same evening, I told my husband I wanted to meet the baby. He left, went and got the child and I asked to hold him; he was so precious. I stared at him looking for a resemblance to his dad, which I never saw. Then the baby started crying but I just held on to him; the cause of my pain and brokenness. There was nothing in the world that he or anyone could say to me to cheer me up.

I heard so many stories of how he had brought the child to my brother's home and said he was just helping out his friend. I later learned through him that he was tired of hiding the child when the mother asked him to keep him. He explained that he had made up in his mind to tell me about the child, but my friend beat him to the punch.

His Excuse

Johnny's explanation was; "Being away from you for almost two years got me feeling lonely, and it was like this situation presented itself and it just happened. Things had gotten hard and I had to go live with my cousins and their mom, who years earlier had opened their home up to this young lady whose mother were friends with my cousin's mother. It was never a real relationship. It was that she started confiding in me. I reached out to her and that is how it all started; it was not like I planned it. She had always known how much I loved you and I would never leave you."

How can you love someone and still hurt them? Yea, yea, yea, gullible as I am, I could not digest that story. I could understand him being lonely but the rest, no way. Diseases are so easily contracted, and anyone can have a deadly disease and you would not have a clue they did. How can you be playing around with someone unprotected? Wasn't he thinking of his health or mine? You can't just look at someone and assume they have great health. I guess they both just threw caution to the wind. I believe they just said, "Hey let us have a good time and whatever happens, happens." I could be dead wrong but that is exactly what their actions said. Proverbs 6:27 states, "Can a man take fire in his bosom and his clothes not be burned?" Johnny painted a pretty picture playing the innocent victim that was pranced on by the big bad wolf. He went into this with his eyes wide open and fully aware of what he was getting into. I guess the thrill of someone much younger than him appealed to his masculinity.

That first night and the week that followed, we were like total strangers lying in bed together, yet apart. I briefly mentioned the many conflicting emotions I was feeling. There were so many times I just wanted him to pull me close and never let me go and other times the sight of him caused my stomach to churn. My family did everything in their power to make me comfortable and so the tears, were not as frequent as before.

I recall him telling me, "Suzie, if you cannot deal with it you can go, I just don't want to see you miserable anymore." At first, I got mad because I misunderstood his statement and the quarrelling began. How could he say that to me? I just wanted him to make this nightmare go away. I never wanted to have to deal with this mess. I wanted him to suffer and cry like I was crying so I could see the physical signs that he was hurting too but he held everything in. After speaking with hurting women, it dawned on me that we are far more emotional than men. I did not know then that the anguish of losing me was eating him up because he played it so cool. I later found out that he didn't know what I would do, so he was only trying to protect himself in case I decided to end our marriage. He was being cautious so as not to show too much emotions. Oh, I wanted to slap him.

My sister-in-law kept asking when we were going to meet this other woman. She so wanted to be there to defend me should it get physical.

The Meeting

He said he wanted our marriage, so I summed up the courage and decided I was ready to meet this young woman. He had no choice but to take me to see her. Sometimes our husbands are such cowards for want of a better word, because this woman had no clue I would be coming with my husband to meet her. Apparently, she had called him to pick her up from work, which I found out was kind of like the normal thing he did, so he used that opportunity to his advantage. She had no clue I would be there with him.

I remember him driving up to this Jerk Machine business place and parking. We sat outside in the car until she locked up and came out. Of course she walked up to the front passenger side to open the door. When she saw me, she went to sit in the back seat behind me. She was a beautiful, much younger, thinner, light skinned, long hair woman. The exact image I mentioned that the Lord showed me in the previous chapter. Let me describe myself. I'm rather beautiful, full figured and dark skinned, the complete opposite. Bouts of insecurity flooded my mind because my husband had always complained of my weight gain, but I wasn't about to fold up here.

He introduced us, "Suzie this is Patsy (not her real name)." We both said hello to each other, and the conversation went on. I learned through her that they had been seeing each other for a period of four years; how could she not love him?

I remember asking them both a few questions but the one that stands out in my mind is this one; "So Johnny tell me. Don't think of me as your wife now, think of me as the other mother of one of your children and choose tonight who you want to be with?" He had been telling me, he made a mistake and he wants his marriage, but all this was done without the other party present. So now that all three of us were finally together he had to publicly choose.

This was his response, "I made my choice years ago and I am going to stick with it."

I asked again, "What is your choice?" because if you agree with me, what he said wasn't clear.

He then said, "My choice is my wife." Patsy never had much more to say after that, so we brought her home. My sister-in-law was mad when I told her I met his baby-mother[1] and she missed out on all the excitement. It was a rather brief meeting that went quite smoothly. I never knew it was going to get ugly.

The Calls

The screened calls continued. According to him, he knew the hurt was still too raw and he was trying to protect me. If after he publicly chose me, why was there still a need for private conversations? Apparently Patsy was not ready to let go. She started making rude phone calls demanding he still picked her up from work because she needed to get home to their son. They were an item. I tell you; they must have had something good going on.

He never brought the child back to the house because he said if I never wanted to see him again he would understand. Patsy had met his sisters, and his aunt. They went to church together and now that it was coming to an end and it seemed like missy was not ready to give up without a showdown. When things grew worse with the annoying phone calls, I had to get her aunt involved, even though I had not met her before. I finally met his cousin's mom. By the way and Johnny introduced me to her when we ran into her at the grocery store. It was not her place, but I asked her to kindly tell her niece to get on with her life because her chapter in mine had come to an end.

That one conversation I had with her aunt started a lifelong friendship with her and her family. I met the rest of her family and to my surprise they were quite nice to me, and up until this day, we have a beautiful friendship. According to what I learned, she had told her niece that Johnny was a married man with a Christian wife, and she needed to stay out of our marriage. I guess that was to no avail.

Her calls kept coming and it went on for a while. There was a lot of disrespect on her end, where I would answer his phone call and she would hang up. Johnny was trying so hard to regain my trust and so the screened calls eventually had come to an end. I clearly remember we were in another state when she called demanding him to purchase some things for their son. He shared it with me and I told her he would get her one of the items but not everything and that we now no longer had secrets between us so she needs to stop; she hung up on me. I waited patiently for her to call again because

I was going to serve her one of the same dishes she has always served me.

She called a few days later not knowing we had a plan for her. My husband and I planned that when she called again, he would answer the call then hand the phone over to me. He did exactly that, answered her and handed me the phone and I got my chance. I was rude to her on this one occasion and a feeling of momentary satisfaction came over me. All this time I was being the quiet un-confrontational wife, but I just about had it with her rudeness. After that, she didn't call him for a while. There is a common saying, "Hurt people, hurt people." Well, deep inside I was still hurting and filled with unforgiveness, so I didn't put my Christian teachings first. I wanted her to hurt too.

I wanted my husband to hurt too. Up until this point, he still had no clue I was unfaithful to him. I wanted him to pay, so I started plotting how I was going to sleep with my friend who I mentioned in an earlier chapter again and this time openly; to get back at him when I got back home. Isn't it sad that when some of us are hurting, we believe that the only way to get back some kind of satisfaction is to serve back what was served to us? We want to get even, even if it leaves a bad taste in our mouth. Carnality is cruel, self-seeking and destructive. Galatians 5:16 states, "So I say walk by the spirit and you will not gratify the desires of the flesh."

I am a minister of the gospel and the church I attended when I was in the United States would always ask me to minister in their services. You will not believe what I am about to say. Patsy and her family were now attending this church. Can you imagine how I felt sitting across the aisle seeing her walk in Sunday after Sunday? Sometimes he would be there and the child would come over to sit with us. I felt like a complete fool, but I played it pretty cool until... This particular morning after church, the Holy Spirit decided he wanted to have a serious conversation with me. I was not looking forward to this.

"Figuratively speaking, it was like putting a leash on a dog."

CHAPTER FOUR

My Inner Feelings

"Out of the fire to the flames of another trial, when you feel like your heart has had all it can take and nothing is there left to break; in the heat of the fire, God will cool you when you don't understand. He is tried and true, no matter the question, there is an answer for you."

- Babbie Mason

Romans 8:28 - "And we know that all things work together for good to them that love God, to them who are called according to His purpose."

Seeing them on Sundays made my insecurity grow, even though I now had my husband back. I kept thinking, "These people in this Church must think I am a complete fool." Yet no one ever had the boldness to voice it aloud which made me think they must be laughing behind my back waiting for me to break.

Everyone knew I had only one biological son and now to openly accept this child as my son everyone would know the story. I wondered how much more of this I could take, when would I eventually break? There is a saying that goes, "Out of sight, out of mind;" I am convinced that there is some truth to this statement. Every time I saw them the wound would again become so raw, and the pain would come back with such a brutal force that I am amazed I held myself together. I know what it is like to put on a show outwardly and to be secretly dying inwardly. I knew I had to get to a place where I would eventually have to let my marriage go to once again find some kind of solace, or to forgive them. It was the only way I would begin to have peace of mind and allow myself to heal the way God intended. It is so hard ministering when you are broken though.

For a while, all I could think was; is it for real, is God accepting this kind of worship when there is unforgiveness reigning in our hearts? Proverbs 4:23

says, "Keep your heart with all diligence for out of your hearts flows the issues of life." This scripture kept playing on my mind. There is a vast difference between being broken and having complete trust in God to take you through the process of whatever you are facing, versus being broken and struggling to forgive. From a spiritual perspective, man is a tripartite being made up of body, soul and spirit, and there is always a constant struggle with the body and soul against the spirit.

We would describe the body and soul as the flesh realm. It consists of our will, our mind, our intellect and our emotions and the spirit as the spiritual realm. It houses the Spirit of God. The body and soul always seek to gratify the flesh and do what pleases it, while the spirit desires to please God and do what the Word says. Your spirit is always in the right place. Now it is your body and soul that needs to come into alignment with what the spirit is in alignment with, to bring about the power of true forgiveness so that you can be effective in your ministry. In truth, you cannot be very impactful and minister to your fullest potential until there is total forgiveness.

There were times I was so angry with Johnny that I made unfair demands of him. I did not know that I was secretly becoming a manipulator and a nag, and I did not care about his feelings. I was so jealous and constantly kept tabs on him; figuratively speaking, it was like putting a leash on a dog. That was what I was doing to my husband, and all this I was unaware of until much later. Ladies, do not do that to your husbands; it will drive them away from you. I was driving him away from me because I was allowing unforgiveness to eat me up.

This went on for years, I remember my self-esteem got so low, that one day my brother Robert, had to take me before the mirror, stood me up and said, "Look at you! You are beautiful, do not allow Johnny to do this to you." Then he jokingly added, "If I was not your brother, I would *draw for you*[2]." That put a smile on my face.

I always felt the stares of others just wanting to hear the story behind my stepson, the unasked questions. It could have been a mind over matter feeling but, truth be told, if the shoe was on another sister's foot, I would want to hear the details behind the story.

"*The Holy Spirit's voice was so sharp in His rebuke, that for a while I was left speechless.*"

CHAPTER FIVE

The Healing Process Began

I think it finally dawned on her that the love affair was over, and we were not as hostile to each other as we were at first. I honestly believed that in the beginning I was showing more ownership of my husband and I wanted that message to be clear to her; you have had your fun, now it is time to back down. Now looking back, I can understand why she refused to let go even after hearing my husband said he chose me.

He made a baby with her, and now he just wanted to leave her hanging, hell I would have put up a fight too. Who knew what kind of promises he had made to her? Who knew if he had promised to leave me for her; who knows? He said he never gave her that kind of assurance, because these were some of the questions I asked. But then he also said he was not seeing anyone when I asked him how he was coping with my absence.

I oftentimes prayed and asked God to help me to forgive my husband and Patsy and thought I really did. Yet, whenever I saw her and the child, I felt like someone was stabbing me in my back all over again and I knew I was still having a problem dealing with it. I thought, *how am I ever going to get over this?*

She continued calling of course because her child had to be taken care of. Eventually we became a bit more courteous to each other over the months that ensued. I told her, this child was a part of my family and as much as I did not like it, I wanted to get to know him. It was one of the best decisions I ever made. I asked to see the child because I wanted to form a bond with him, and by now I could speak peaceably with his mom.

Patsy sometimes asked me to pick her son up from school so we could spend time together, but I was not totally delivered. The screened calls stopped but I still had my insecurities dealing with. If my husband went to pick up the child, he would ask me to come with him because he wanted to put my fears to rest. I would tag along and as parents, Patsy and I became courteous to each other for the sake of the child. If anyone asked me during this time, was I able to trust him again? It would have been a definite no.

I went back home to the islands after almost staying for five months only to return a year later to permanently live.

* * *

So now it is the Monday following the Sunday I heard in my spirit, "I want to have a serious conversation with you." I experienced God's love in such a powerful way that it has left an indelible print on my mind. I got up like I normally do, I am a Recording Artist, so I love to sing; I sing without thinking of it. I got into singing and praising, and this is the encounter I had.

The Holy Spirit's voice was so sharp in His rebuke, that for a while I was left speechless. He said and I quote, "I am tired of the pity party. I know you are hurting. I have felt your pain, now get over it!" It was a direct command and the next step I took would determine how I lived the remainder of my life. It was decision making time.

I remember when King David committed adultery and Bathsheba got pregnant and gave birth to the baby who became ill. He began to fast in hope that God would heal the child. He did this for a number of days and when the news came that the baby died the king got up, showered himself, worshipped and ate. You can read this in 2nd Samuel: 12:16-20.

Hearing this message, my first thought was, *God you are insensitive; I'm hurting here.* But because He has supreme control over my life, He did not want the prolonged pity party. He had more than had enough. I could not believe that God Himself was tired of the tears and my feeling sorry for myself. If it bothered God, can you tell me how much my husband who doesn't have a shade of God's patience must have felt? No wonder he told me if I could not deal with it, I could leave him. I seriously had no clue I was doing this.

The encounter did not stop there, it went on for hours. The next thing I heard was, "Gird up your loins for your journey is still great, and if you can't get over this, then I can't take you any further." This was a serious wakeup call. I had to let go of whatever I was holding on to. I am no match for God. I then remembered Elijah in 1ˢᵗ Kings 18:46, "And the hand of the Lord was on Elijah, and he gathered up his garment and he ran before Ahab to the entrance of Jezreel." I believe the healing began after this experience. Not only did I need to forgive Johnny and Patsy for committing adultery, I also to accept a child and call him my own. This was when

I began to experience the power of true forgiveness and healing. It was a process, that could no longer be delayed, but I can truly say that I began to let go and let God.

I honestly do not believe that true forgiveness can be experienced by one who has no relationship with God. It is okay if you disagree with me, but like I briefly mentioned earlier about the soul and the body, they seek only to gratify the flesh. It will always want to hold on to the pain and seek ways to inflict hurt where it has been hurt and get some kind of sick satisfaction out of doing it as well. My advice to you, "Do not do it." This feeling will not last. It will constantly drive you to cause more harm than good. It is momentary satisfaction that will bring future regret.

Have you ever heard someone say, "If I had made a better decision I would not have been in this mess?" I honestly cannot take any credit for how God brought me through. But looking back now, I can tell you some of the steps, as to how I got here. What I can truly tell you is that one has to have a heart, and an ear that will be receptive to hearing God's voice and moving in the direction of obedience to honor what He has spoken. We cannot do it in our own strength.

There were days when I thought I was over this mess and like a cannon ball it would come back and rock my world. It takes the spirit of God and a willingness on your part to achieve what I have achieved. I overcame this and so can you. God will have to help you through it; there is no way around this.

The Closure to Unforgiveness

Migrating after a year, I was back in The States with my son. The relationship with my stepson, let me call him Mark, grew. I told Patsy I needed both boys to develop a relationship, even though Jay-R was nine years older, so he stayed with us on weekends. Soon after we migrated, my husband gave his heart to the Lord. He was hardly home due to his job in another State so I was mostly on my own.

I wrote this in a journal a year later and accidentally came upon it while I was writing this book.

Dated October 25, 2008

Dear diary, on this day I write the truth about my stepson. Surprisingly, everyone with the exception of my family knew the pain and the suffering I went through finding out I was a stepmom, and not even they knew the depth of what I was going through.

You see people can be around you, yet you are still lonely. There is the fear of them not being able to handle the harshness of your truth, your reality. I felt cheap, used not good enough. Mark was born in July 2004. To everyone who had the courage to ask me how I coped with it and thought I was very brave and had it all together, secretly I was an emotional wreck. The truth of the matter was, I really wanted to scream, hit somebody, walk out on my husband really. I just wanted to die. I believe I mentioned this in an earlier chapter.

The church I attended before I came to live here is where Patsy's family started worshipping. Can you believe the nerve of her? It was like a slap in my face every Sunday seeing her. Worship for me became a drag. It was like every time I would walk into the church my eyes would be searching for her. Did all this make me hate my husband? No, it didn't, but I pretty much wanted to. He tried to comfort me as best as he could, but I refused to be comforted.

My whole self-esteem dropped from a 100% to about a 40. I started questioning how I looked; criticizing my weight gain. My family members kept telling me how beautiful I am which was altogether true but I just could not see the outer beauty much less the inner. I thought of how I had cheated which had left me unsatisfied and hating me even more.

How could I compete with someone much younger, slimmer and very attractive? Up until this point, I wasn't totally convinced that my husband still loved me. How could you love someone, hurt them, then turn around and ask her to leave if it made her feel better? Insensitive is what he was.

The pain was not as bad as it was the previous year, but I was still not delivered. I had gotten closer to Mark but to say I truly loved him as my own up to this point would be a lie. I cared for him but I sometimes I wished he did not belong to my husband. I even asked my husband if he had ever thought of doing a D.N.A. test because he said Patsy denied that she was pregnant when he confronted her. You see he had moved away from the house to another State so he too had his doubts. I wanted something to prove he didn't belong to him which he was willing to do but never got around to doing.

I was confused, he was confused because this minute I was fine the next minute I was not. I finally said to hell with the DNA if he hadn't slept with her, she could not have called his name, so I forgot about that. I felt like I was being scrutinized when I took him out. Most people around me knew the story, so when strangers would ask, "Is he your son?" I would say no because I had not yet accepted him as such. I so wanted to get past the looks when they heard him call my husband, Dad, but it got much harder before it got better.

Whenever mark came over, I would give him baths, brush his teeth, lotion his skin, brush his hair, dress him, hug him and pray with him. Deep down I felt like a fraud. I felt stupid for doing this. I asked myself, "Am I doing this for him, his dad or for me?" I felt obligated somehow and hated the feeling. I felt like distancing myself from this child would be better for me, but I was trying to do the Christian thing. He was a constant reminder of what I thought I would never have again, another child to hug, cuddle and give all my love, my son was almost thirteen by this time. How do I handle this pain?

I so desired to leave this all behind me. I wished it never happened but it did. Yet through all these mixed emotions I felt so protective of him. He was like a breakable jar and I didn't want him to be hurt by all this. I knew the child was innocent and he didn't ask to be born into this world, yet knowing this didn't make the pain any easier to bear.

All this time God was healing me. I had totally forgotten the revelation I had about "Standing in the gap.'" I was so busy pointing the finger that I didn't realize it was pointing back at me. One day it suddenly hit me that in some strange way I was partly responsible because I had failed to live up to the principles of God's word concerning my marriage to my husband. That was when I began to feel some peace in the whole mess. Please do not ask me to explain this. I just felt like my failure resulted in his failure.

Yes, I did tell Johnny I committed adultery. He was quite upset, but funny enough, he handled this situation pretty well. I guess because I had no evidence of a child it was easier for him to deal with. He demanded to talk to this young man mentioned in an earlier chapter and he did, but he just kept on loving me. There were times I would see him looking at me and I knew he was remembering what I did to him and I would ask him to let it go and he would just hold me. It was hard for him because he held me in such high regards, and no one could tell him anything bad about me. He simply would not believe.

I really broke his trust when I told him I slept with this young man. I knew he was hurting but he never made me feel like he no longer wanted me. I was told never to talk with this young man again. I argued of course because to me he was more of a friend than a lover but we had crossed the line and I guess for us to have peace reign in our home I obliged, unwillingly. This young man I was never emotionally attached to. Yes, we had sex and that is where we crossed the line, but he and I had a mutual understanding that we could never be more than friends. I never gave him any hope that I would leave my husband. I remember when Johnny made the call to him, and made it clear that he knew what happened between him and I. He admitted it and said it should not have happened but it did, and Johnny strongly suggested he let it stay where it was hidden. My husband was defending my honour. That is love, and I was so glad that I confessed and told him about my unfaithfulness. He handled it far better than I thought he would.

I believed, for anything broken to be mended one has to come clean and lay it all on the table, then begin to work from there. We both needed to be whole again, especially me.

"It was like immediately when I released them the miracle took place. I was free, healed, and delivered."

CHAPTER SIX

How I knew I was completely Healed

*"I've been changed, freed, healed, and delivered.
I've found joy, peace, grace and favour.
Right now, is the moment today is the day I've been
changed, I've been changed I have waited for this
moment to come and I won't let it pass me by."*

- William McDowell

After that encounter with the Holy Spirit I knew I had to take the necessary steps to being healed. A broken heart can lead to so many physical illnesses like depression, inflicting hurt on oneself, high blood pressure, drug addiction, one becoming an alcoholic and even suicide; if one does not seek the help they need. Brokenness can cause one to become physically abusive to others, fits of uncontrolled anger and outburst. Getting medical help is just a temporary relief because we are just dealing with the symptoms and not the cause. We need a cure, so we need to find the root cause of the problem, and then, and only then, will we be able to cure the pain. I no longer wanted a quick fix; I wanted a cure.

My healing process began earlier the same year through text messaging. This was our conversation, I wrote it down; the words Patsy and I shared with each other five years ago.

Me: "For the hurt you and my husband have caused me I truly forgive you."

Patsy: "Thank you, I needed that."

Me: "If you ever need to talk, I am here to listen. As much as I wanted to hate you, I can't. I love you and pray that you will find the happiness you deserve, God bless you."

Patsy: "I pray that for what I have done to your relationship no one else would try. Because what I have been through is nothing and if I never told you, I am very sorry. If you only knew just because of what I have done it is so hard for me to find someone to love me for me and not my body but now I know, thanks for forgiving me." *Conversation ends.*

The transformation was immediate. Right then and there I felt like a bird, so light. I felt as if I had wings, as if I could soar. I felt as if a ton of bricks was lifted from my shoulders. I could finally breathe again.

Then I placed the next call to my husband who was working out of State and told him, "I have forgiven Patsy and I forgive you too." My joy came flooding back like a river. I had found the peace that I had lost over the years. I was whole again. Glory be to God! All it finally took was a made-up mind and I was ready. I had enough. Jesus was there waiting to restore me unto Himself, but He would not forcibly take from me that which He wanted me to willingly give up. If He had to force me to forgive it would not be a sacrifice. A sacrifice has to cost you something, it cost Him His life. I had to make the sacrifice to become whole again. After all, I was the one who had everything to gain or to lose. I chose to win.

Unforgiveness is really heavy and oh the relief you'll feel when you begin to walk in forgiveness. I immediately felt such peace, a peace that this long arduous journey of unforgiveness was finally over. It was not an easy journey, but it was finally over. It was like immediately when I released them the miracle took place. I was free, healed, and delivered. Now I am completely healed. You ask me, how can you be so sure you're delivered from unforgiveness? and this is my answer, "There is no more pain, no more bitterness, no more anger, and no more insecurity.

Winning this Battle

I mentioned in chapter one that I was the baby in my family and so people would think twice of messing with me. I came after three boys, and they were not afraid to rough anyone up who tried to hurt me. I was never a kid who made trouble, so they never had to physically defend me from anyone. Still, I always knew if I needed them, they would be there.

I remember when I just started dating Johnny, this one girl was sending threats to me because I guess she was still hung up on him. Johnny made it quite clear to her not to mess with me, and I made sure to relate the matter to my brothers, I have always had them in my corner. The infidelity in my marriage was the very first battle I had to really fight and it was not a physical one. My brothers could not help me. Maybe I could have asked my brothers to rough up my husband a bit but what would that have proven or where would it have gotten me? Maybe bailing someone out of jail or burying someone, because he would have not gone down without a fight.

Here is a nugget, "Physical weapons cannot fight spiritual wars." I had to fight this one on my own and not even in my strength but only through the strength of the Holy Spirit. I had to learn that physical weapons cannot fight spiritual wars. He had to teach my spirit to war and prepare me to win this battle.

Now I had forgiven, trust had to be rebuilt, and here is where I started. It finally dawned on me that there are steps to accomplishing goals, and my constant presence hovering over him would not stop him if he decided he was going to cheat. I apprehensively made my next step. I stopped accompanying Johnny to pick Mark up. I was learning my steps and because I knew that for trust to be re-established in our lives, I would have to start somewhere, I chose to start here. Sometimes Johnny and I would sit around and laugh about how things were. When he and Patsy had run-ins, I would jokingly ask him, "What were you thinking fooling around with a girl fourteen years your junior? What did you expect?" He would only shake his head and smile.

If anyone had asked me at the beginning if it was even possible to be able to look back on the thing that caused the greatest pain and smile about it, I would have told them it was impossible, but that's how the God I know operates. He specializes in the things that are impossible and makes them possible. For us to walk in completeness, Jesus, the only begotten Son of the Father, had to be broken. Though He never physically had any broken bones according to Bible prophecy, Calvary's cross was the significant turning point that brought back hope, restoration and redemption to mankind. He made that possible. Oh hallelujah!

Jay had hang-ups about his little brother but deep down I think he was jealous that I could grow to love Mark so selflessly. He'd oftentimes accuse me of taking his side and would remind me he is not mine. When he'd do that, I'd tell him that Mark has as much right in our home as he does, so not to make the mistake of thinking he is more special. The battle between sibling rivalry remained for years and is still present but minimal. Sometimes he'd allow him to play his games, but this was very rare. I have learnt over the years to not pay too much attention to them. He has never been abusive to him. Growing up he'd just tune him out most of the times. Mark would spend every holiday with us and mostly every weekend.

The bond between both boys hasn't really deepened after all these years. I think the age gap between them plays a factor and I also believe that Jon-Ross still has not gotten over the fact that his Dad had a child that was not ours. He, however, no longer tells Mark I am not his Mom when he sometimes calls me Mommy. Our sons, sadly I believe, still has a long way to go with their relationship. I believe they care much for each other in their own way though. They communicate occasionally when Mark comes over if he is here but that is just about it.

As for me and Mark, he grew on me so much and took such a liking to me, that I had no choice but to return his love. We have a great relationship. I have always known he was innocent and not to be blamed for my pain, but it was not easy reaching out and loving him as my own until I had truly forgiven my husband and his mother. When I introduce Mark as my son and they say, "I thought you had only one son."

I now proudly say, "Oh he's my husband's," and I don't care anymore about the raised eyebrows and the questions they so badly want to ask. Mark is my love child; his mom and I have a good relationship. I no longer wonder how or why this happened. I now know there was purpose for my pain.

I kept asking God to heal me, but I had a major role to play in letting the pain go. I needed peace with myself and those around me and I found that peace when I released myself from the prison walls I had built around myself. I was able to love and trust others again. The great Iconic Jamaican singer the legendary Bob Marley said, "Emancipate yourself from mental slavery, none but ourselves can free our minds." Hallelujah! I now walk in complete and total forgiveness; praises be to God. Hallelujah!

1ˢᵗ Corinthians 13 states;

"[1]If I speak in the tongues of men and of angels, but have not love, I am only a resounding gong or a clanging cymbal. [2]If I have the gift of prophecy and can fathom all mysteries and all knowledge, and if I have a faith that can move mountains, but have not love, I am nothing. [3]If I give all I possess to the poor and surrender my body to the flames, but have not love, I gain nothing. [4]Love is patient, love is kind. It does not envy, it does not boast, it is not proud. [5]It is not rude, it is not self-seeking, it is not easily angered, keeps no record of wrongs. [6]Love does not delight in evil but rejoices with the truth. [7]It always protects, always trusts, always hopes, always persevere. [8]Love never fails. But where there are prophecies, they will cease; where there are tongues, they will be stilled; where there is knowledge, it will pass away. [9]For we know in part and we prophesy in part, [10]but when perfection comes, the imperfect disappears. [11]When I was a child, I talked like a child I thought like a child, I reasoned like a child. When I became a man, I put childish ways behind me. [12]Now we see but a poor reflection as in a mirror; then we shall see face to face. Now I know in part; then I shall know fully, even as I am fully known. [13]And now these three remain: faith, hope and love. But the greatest of these is love.

"I have come to understand that forgiveness is not about how badly you have been hurt."

EPILOGUE

"Through it all, through it all
I've learned to trust in Jesus, I've learned to trust
in God
Through it all, through it all
I've learned to depend upon his word."
-     Andrae Crouch

Life sometimes throws you a curve ball and leaves you in a state of bewilderment. Bewilderment defined is, "The condition of being confused or disoriented. Or, a situation of perplexity or confusions tangled." Unforgiveness left me in such a cold, dark, lonely place. Understand that I had expressed my desire to have another child, which eventually happened. Even though I had given birth to our son, my two pregnancies were not exactly alike. They are different, but I still felt like Hannah in 1st Samuel chapter 1. Here is a synopsis of the story so you can clearly understand where I am going with this.

There was this man named Elkanah who had two wives, Hannah and Peninah. Hannah was barren and Peninah had children. It was said that the husband loved Hannah more than Peninah and would give her double portions, much more than the other wife. Yet it was not sufficient for Hannah; she wanted a child of her own. This woman would mock and provoke her just to irritate her because she was childless. She would flaunt her children in her face and it always reduced Hannah to tears. Then one day, she went to the temple and cried out to God, who not only heard her but answered her prayer. She later gave birth to one of the greatest Prophet that ever lived, a boy named Samuel.

Peninah in my life also represented pain that just kept on going and going but not only her. Mark was a constant reminder of what I thought I would never have again. In my case I needed to cry out to God by letting go of my pain and forgive everyone caught up in our situation. When I did, I got my female version of Samuel. In November 2012, I gave birth to her, her name is Jhireh Esther-Jade Walker. She represents the Provision, the Faithfulness and the Power of Almighty God. I had to let everything go so he could heal me and give me the child of my promise. Though you are thrown a curved ball and you want to give up, your spirit is telling you just to push a little harder.

Your situation may not be the same as mine but whatever it is that has led you to this place of bitterness, anger, hatred, jealousy, bondage, unforgiveness, think seriously; who is it hurting? It is not the other party, it is you. It is putting a barrier between you and your God. Sometimes the people that have hurt us do not even remember they did us wrong, yet we keep holding on to the pain. Unforgiveness is giving people power over you. The only person that should have that control is God, take it back from them.

You say, how do they have power over me? They take away your peace of mind. They mess with your prayers being answered. They make you see others as untrustworthy. You say, I am dealing with it. I say, how? By not talking to them, ignoring them because this will keep them away from you; is that God's way?

I ask you today whoever it is that has you in this place of bondage, because whether you believe it or not that is what unforgiveness is, say this prayer with me.

"Lord, I release (insert their names here) this day and I ask that you help me to let go of every hurt and anger I hold towards them. Set me free and create in me a clean heart oh God and renew a right spirit within me. In Jesus' name, Amen.

Isaiah 59:1-2 states, "'Behold, the Lord's hand is not shortened, that it cannot save; neither his ear heavy, that it cannot hear: 'But your iniquities have separated between you and your God, and your sins have hid his face from you, that he will not hear."

Patsy is now a married woman and our friendship blossomed into that of me being like a big sister, giving her advice in her marriage, her Christianity and parenting. This was spoken prophetically to her by my husband years before and she told me when we became friends that she told him he was crazy, and I would be a fool to talk to her. I smile when at this. Becoming who God has created me to be, I believe, propelled me into doing what I did next.

My husband was incarcerated for a short time, and around the same time of his incarceration she started experiencing financial difficulties. Her husband had lost his job and she had to move from her place of abode. Not knowing where she would be living, she thought of renting an efficiency unit to house her, her nephew and husband. She told me I had to take Mark until she was back on her feet again. I had no problem with taking him, but his school was a little distant from where I lived. That was my only issue and she did not want him to change schools. After thinking about her dilemma, I told my husband I was going to have them stay with us until she got another place. I wanted to help so that the money she would be paying for rent could actually be saved up for somewhere more convenient for her and her family. He thought I was crazy, but he said if I was sure I wanted to do that it was up to me. I shared it with my son and he objected at first, then later agreed. You see, we were by ourselves and I wanted him to remain comfortable in our home.

I told Patsy she could stay with us if it wouldn't make her uncomfortable and she said she would discuss it with her husband. After about a week, she took me up on the offer. There were other offers made from her church folks but her husband, for reasons I don't know, told her he would prefer if she stayed with me, while he stayed by his dad. They moved into our home. I had not discussed this with my family members or friends and when they found out they raised the roof. Some said I was stupid. Others said, "You did not think this through properly. How could you have her in your house?" Some thought she still had feelings for my husband and she would hurt me. I heeded to none of their concerns because I felt in my spirit I was doing the right thing.

We had no problems in my household during the time she lived there and she helped out as much as she could. My only problem was she did not like to cook (laughing out loud). She said she never liked cooking, so I continued cooking because we all had to eat. I included her when I had to visit my husband's lawyer; after all, she had a child for him too. I hid nothing from her about his case and even asked her to go visit him for me when I was unable to, but she never did. He spent four months and 21 days behind bars, and she moved out the same day he got released.

Against everyone's concern, I followed my heart and was extremely glad I could have helped her in her time of need. Would she have done the same for me is not my concern. I did not do it to prove anything to anyone. I did it because if I was ever in this situation, I would want someone to reach out and help me. People who knew she stayed at my house are still amazed I allowed it, others saw the Christ behind it, and still others, my stupidity.

Now I am sometimes the mediator between Patsy and Johnny. There are times, when she has every reason to be mad at Johnny, and she lets him have it. I sometimes step in between them and cool down the fire. She really is a beautiful young lady and my prayer for her is that she will have a love that lasts forever and never have to go through the pain of unforgiveness and betrayal. She is a woman of integrity and all she needed was to have a hand of kindness extended to her, wanting nothing in return.

I have come to understand that forgiveness is not about how badly you have been hurt. It's about your willingness to let it go and move beyond the pain and relate to the person or persons with love and acts of kindness expecting nothing in return. I could only have done this through the power of the Holy Spirit because He totally delivered me from the power of unforgiveness.

Patsy and I are still good friends. Johnny got released and I got pregnant after almost eighteen years of giving birth to my son Jay-R. I gave birth to my second biological child Jhireh Esther-Jade. We have three wonderful children. My husband and I are still happily married, and we will be celebrating 21 years of marriage and 30 years of togetherness. God is able, just let him have his perfect way within you and don't drag it out for as long as I did. See you in my next publication.

...Be blessed.

Suzette is a minister and also uses her voice to spread the Word through song. You can listen to her music on YouTube, iTunes and other platforms.

Visit her website today to gain access to her music.

www.suzettegwalker.com

Sometimes talking to someone who knows what you are going through, because they've been there, helps.

Suzette is open to being in touch with women who are dealing with infidelity and can also be contacted through her website in this regard.

A publication by Tamarind Hill Press
www.tamarindhillpress.co.uk

TAMARiND HiLL
.PRESS

CPSIA information can be obtained
at www.ICGtesting.com
Printed in the USA
LVHW090507310721
694023LV00003B/582